SECRETS
OF BEES

For my queen bees,
Tanya, Becky and Louise
— B. H.

For Zachariah
— N. C.

With thanks to Professor Beverley Glover and Dr Sally Lee
from Cambridge University Botanic Garden
for their contribution and advice.

First published 2025 by Nosy Crow Ltd
Wheat Wharf, 27a Shad Thames,
London, SE1 2XZ, UK

Nosy Crow Eireann Ltd
44 Orchard Grove, Kenmare,
Co Kerry, V93 FY22, Ireland

ISBN 978 1 80513 317 9 (HB)
ISBN 978 1 80513 318 6 (PB)

Printed in China following rigorous ethical sourcing standards.

10 9 8 7 6 5 4 3 2 1 (HB)
10 9 8 7 6 5 4 3 2 1 (PB)

SECRETS OF BEES

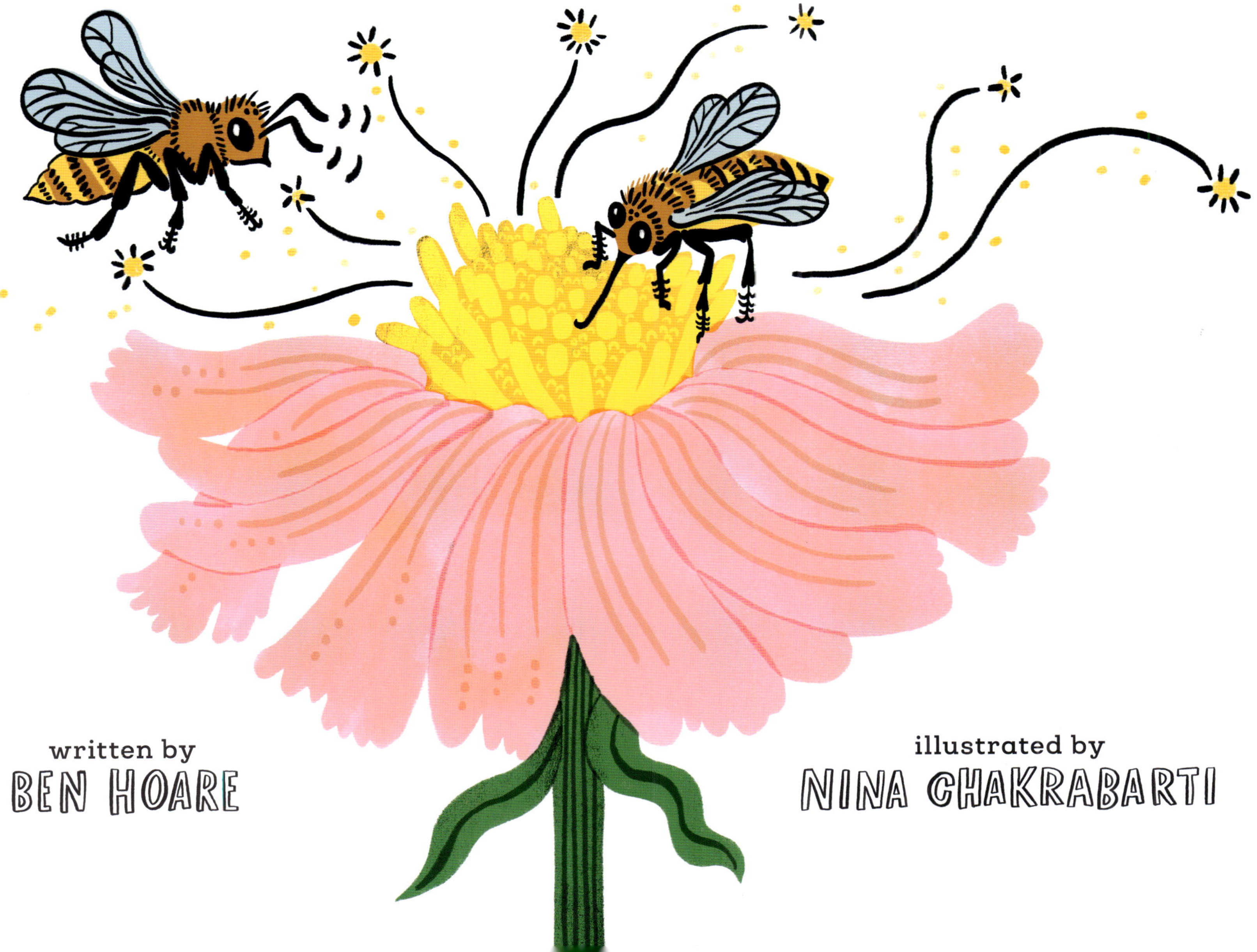

written by
BEN HOARE

illustrated by
NINA CHAKRABARTI

Contents

What is a bee?
Pages 6-7

How many bees are there?
Pages 8-9

What do bees eat?
Pages 10-11

How do bees help plants?
Pages 12-13

What does it feel like to be a bee?
Pages 14-15

How do bees grow up?
Pages 16-17

What happens inside a hive?
Pages 18-19

How do bees make honey?
Pages 20-21

Where do the other bees live?
Pages 22-23

Why do bees have stings?
Pages 24-25

Why do we need bees?
Pages 26-27

How can we help bees?
Pages 28-29

Glossary and Index
Pages 30-32

Introduction

Whenever I notice a bee, I stop what I'm doing and watch.
You see, I just love bees! They are such beautiful, nimble
creatures. They have such intelligent little faces! Bees make
yummy honey too. And, as you will discover in this book,
by flying to and fro they also help to fill our planet with
flowers. There's no doubt about it – bees are BRILLIANT!

Bees have always fascinated people. We have learned so much
about their lives, including how they find food, build nests and
'talk' to each other. But bees still have many secrets. Perhaps
in the future we will solve these mysteries too.

– BEN HOARE

What is a bee?

Bees are brilliant! These amazing creatures have superpowers that we can only dream of. But what actually are bees?

Bees are **invertebrates**, which means they don't have a bony skeleton like humans do. They belong to a large group of invertebrates called insects. All bees share these features:

Tawny mining bee

Wings

Four wings, which are light but strong. When a bee is flying, its wings hook together to make a single pair on each side of its body. Bees can beat their wings around 200 times a second!

Abdomen

A rear body section. Inside are the organs for digesting and breeding.

Stinger

A sharp stinger (female bees only).

Thorax

A middle body section. It contains powerful muscles for flight.

Legs

Six legs, each made of several sections.

Exoskeleton

A tough skin for protection and support, like body armour.

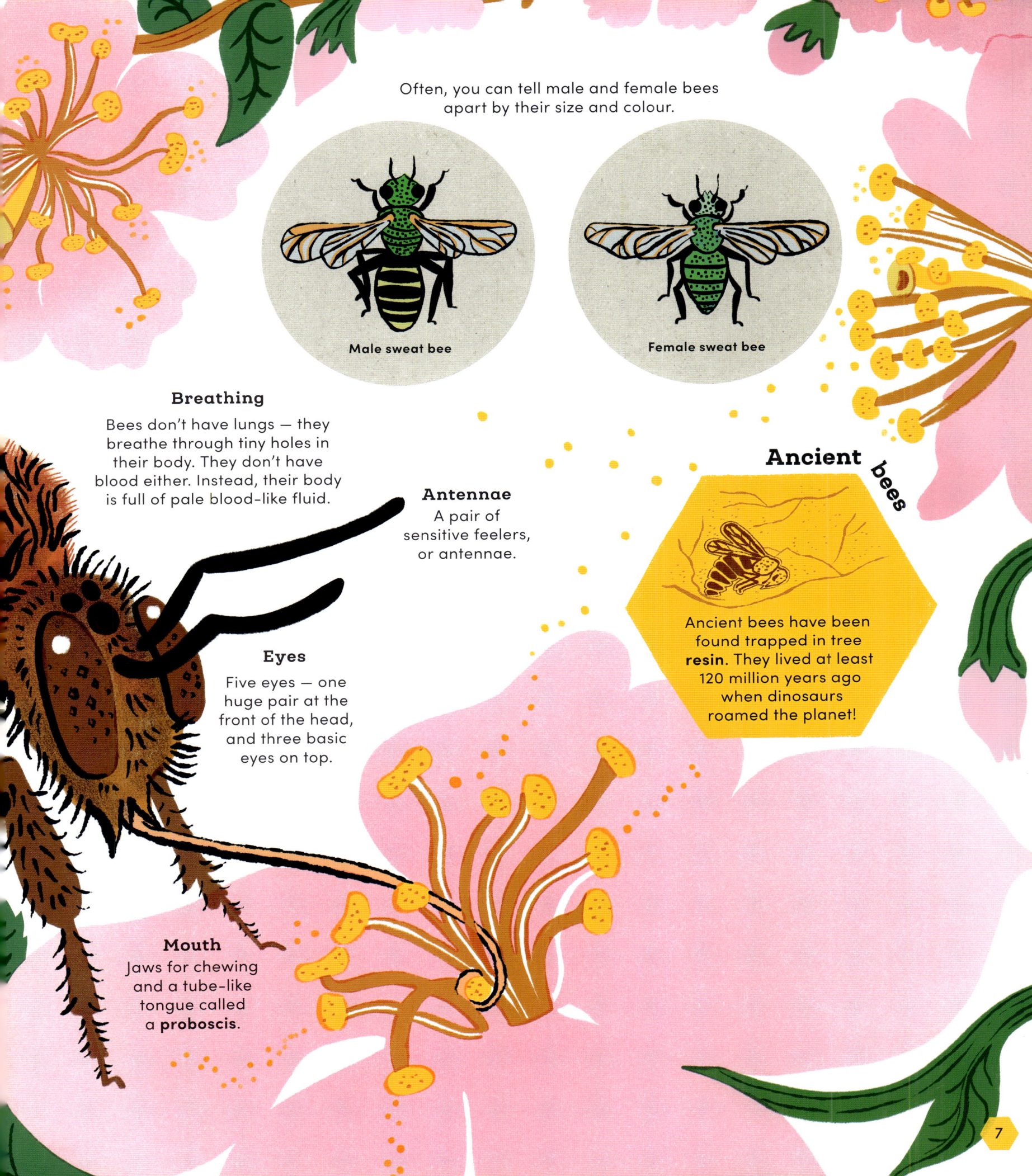

Often, you can tell male and female bees apart by their size and colour.

Male sweat bee

Female sweat bee

Breathing

Bees don't have lungs — they breathe through tiny holes in their body. They don't have blood either. Instead, their body is full of pale blood-like fluid.

Antennae

A pair of sensitive feelers, or antennae.

Eyes

Five eyes — one huge pair at the front of the head, and three basic eyes on top.

Mouth

Jaws for chewing and a tube-like tongue called a **proboscis**.

Ancient bees

Ancient bees have been found trapped in tree **resin**. They lived at least 120 million years ago when dinosaurs roamed the planet!

How many bees are there?

Earth is home to a mind-boggling variety of bees, which come in all sorts of shapes, sizes and colours.

Orchid bee

Long-legged oil bee

Honeybees have a stripy body and are probably the world's best-known bees. But they are just one kind, or **species**, of bee. In fact, there are more than 20,000 different species buzzing around this planet! And these are just the bees we know about so far. Scientists discover new species every year.

Wallace's giant bee

Honeybee

Mini-fairy bee

The biggest bee of all is **Wallace's giant bee**. This humongous bee has a body as long as an adult human's thumb. It lives in **rainforests** in Indonesia and is so rare that few people have ever seen one. The world's smallest bee is the **mini-fairy bee** of the USA, which is just two millimetres long — about the thickness of a grain of rice.

Blue carpenter bee

Did you know that there are even blue bees? One of the bluest is the **blue carpenter bee**.

Orchid cuckoo bee

Many bees glitter like jewels. The shiny effect is not created by **pigment**, which is what gives paint its colour. Instead, these bees are covered in tiny bumps that bounce sunlight around, making their body sparkle.

BZZZzzzz

Bees live in most **habitats** on land. You can even find bees in deserts and in the middle of cities. The only places that *don't* have any bees are tiny islands far out at sea and the icy **continent** of Antarctica.

Cactus bee

White-tailed bumblebee

Bumblebees are so big and furry, they look a little like flying teddy bears! But why are they so hairy? It's because long ago they used to live high in the Himalayas, at a time when the planet was much colder than it is now. The bumblebees developed fur to keep them warm. Today, you can meet bumblebees in many places, including parks and gardens.

What do bees eat?

Bees visit flowers every day to get their two main foods. One is a sweet liquid called nectar. The other is pollen, which looks like powder or dust. Most bees need both nectar and pollen to stay healthy.

Nectar is a mixture of sugar and water that gives bees masses of energy. They suck it out of flowers with their special tongue — a bit like drinking through a straw. Flowers come in many different shapes, and bees have short or long tongues, depending on which types of flowers they visit.

Pollen is packed with all the **protein**, fats, **vitamins** and **minerals** that bees need. Because pollen is gooey, when bees land on a flower, it sticks to the hairs on their legs and body. The bees fly off with it to eat later or feed to their young.

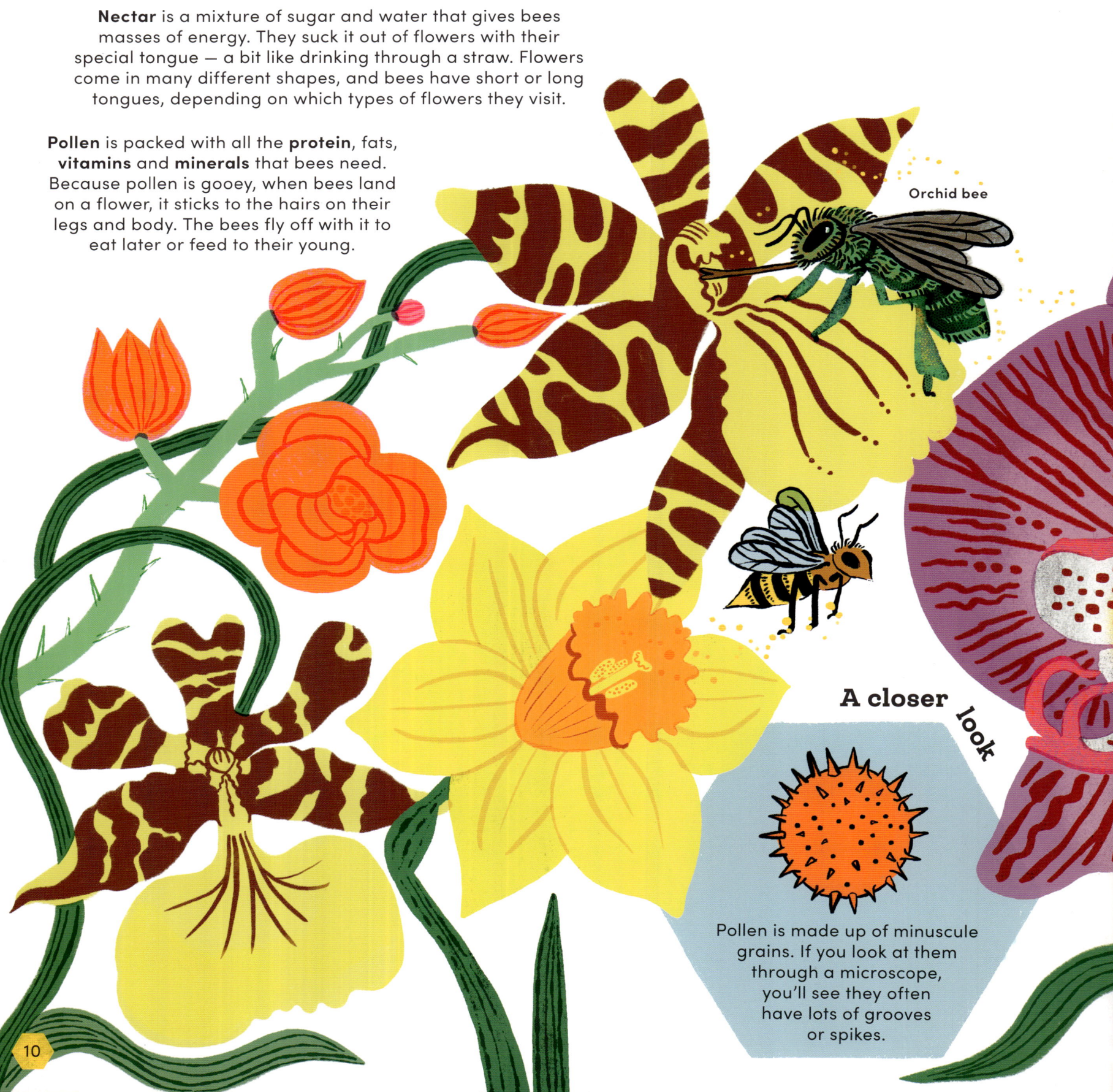

Orchid bee

A closer look

Pollen is made up of minuscule grains. If you look at them through a microscope, you'll see they often have lots of grooves or spikes.

Sweat bees sip the sweat off other animals — including humans! They probably do it because the sweat contains salt and other minerals.

Did you know that bees poo? You may see the droplets pop out of their bottom.

Vulture bees hunt for dead creatures, then feed on the rotting flesh. But they also feed on nectar, like other bees.

Bees LOVE dry, sunny weather. If it's raining, they stop looking for food to avoid getting wet. However, a few unusual bees fly at night and feed from flowers that open after dark!

Indian carpenter bee

How do bees help plants?

Bees are incredibly useful to flowering plants. When they take pollen between the same type of flowering plant, the plants can make seeds. We call this pollination.

The plants need to make seeds because that is how they spread and create new plants. But the bees don't carry the pollen for free. In return for their hard work, the plants give them a reward — sugary nectar. So, both the plants and the bees benefit!

Here's how it works:

1 A bee visits a flower to feed. While it sucks the nectar, pollen from the male part of the flower catches on its body.

Bicolored striped sweat bee

2 Now covered in pollen, the bee flies to another flower.

3 Some of the pollen on its body rubs off as it feeds.

4 This pollen enters the flower, which allows the female part of the flower to make seeds.

Bumblebees also collect pollen by gripping flowers and buzzing. Their wings buzz so hard, it shakes pollen off the flowers onto their body! Bumblebees pollinate several **crops** this way, including tomatoes, potatoes and aubergines.

BuZz

Scientists have discovered that bees have a FANTASTIC memory. Bees need to remember where the best flowers are to help them find the flowers again quickly. So, they create a kind of mental map that shows them exactly where to go — it's like having a satnav in their brain.

BuZz

BuZz

Though bees are great **pollinators**, they are not the only creatures at it. Many other insects pollinate plants, among them butterflies, wasps, beetles and moths. Some birds and bats are also pollinators.

What does it feel like to be a bee?

Bees can see and feel incredible things that are far beyond what we see and feel. Their brain is tiny — no bigger than a full stop — but like a powerful computer it handles masses of information to help them find flowers, escape predators and keep in touch with each other.

Smell

Bees can smell the faintest whiff of chemicals in the air, using their pair of antennae. This helps them to smell which flower is which from far away and pick up scent messages from other bees. It is like speaking a language of scents.

Sight

Bees have huge eyes made up of thousands of minuscule lenses. The image they create is fuzzy, but bees are brilliant at sensing movement and can see all around their head — even what's above, below and behind them. They can see **UV (ultraviolet) light**, too. Many flowers that look plain to us have hidden UV patterns of spots, stripes or circles that act like landing strips, guiding bees to the nectar and pollen. Bees are also able to detect patterns of sunlight in the sky, which help them find their way.

Bees can't see red very well, so flowers that look red to us . . .

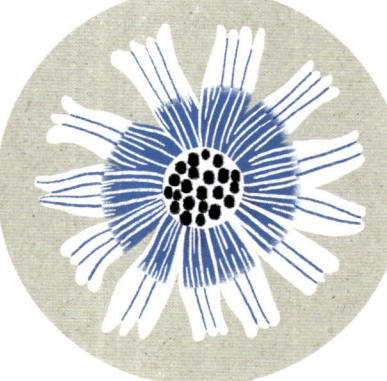

look very different to them!

Hearing

No ears? It's not a problem for bees. They hear with their whole body, feeling the vibrations caused by sound moving through the air. Social bees use vibrations to communicate in the total darkness of their nest.

Think like a bee

Some scientists think bees have feelings, such as pain or happiness. And bees are smart enough to solve puzzles and learn tricks. In a lab, bumblebees were taught to pull on a string to get some nectar, and these trained bees were then able to teach other bumblebees how to do it. Another experiment showed that honeybees can count up to four!

1...2...3...4

Touch

The long hairs covering a bee's body have **nerves** at the base and are highly sensitive to touch. Its antennae are also super-sensitive, and not just to touch, but to tastes and smells as well.

Electro sense

Plants produce weak electrical signals, which some scientists believe bees can detect with their hair. The signals tell them if a flower has already been visited by another bee. If it has, they know it probably has little nectar and pollen left, so they should go to other flowers instead.

How do bees grow up?

Human babies are mini versions of the adult people they grow into. But young bees look *completely different* to adult bees! To become adults, they must go through a dramatic change, which we call metamorphosis.

Bees have four life stages:

1 A bee starts life as an egg laid by a female bee.

2 The egg hatches into a wriggly **larva**, which has no eyes, legs or wings. It eats the food provided – pollen mixed with nectar.

3 Within a week or so, the larva turns into a **pupa**. The pupa doesn't move, but inside, the bee rebuilds its body to change shape.

4 One to two weeks later, the adult bee emerges. Imagine being a bee **larva**. After several days of non-stop eating, you might be 1,500 times larger!

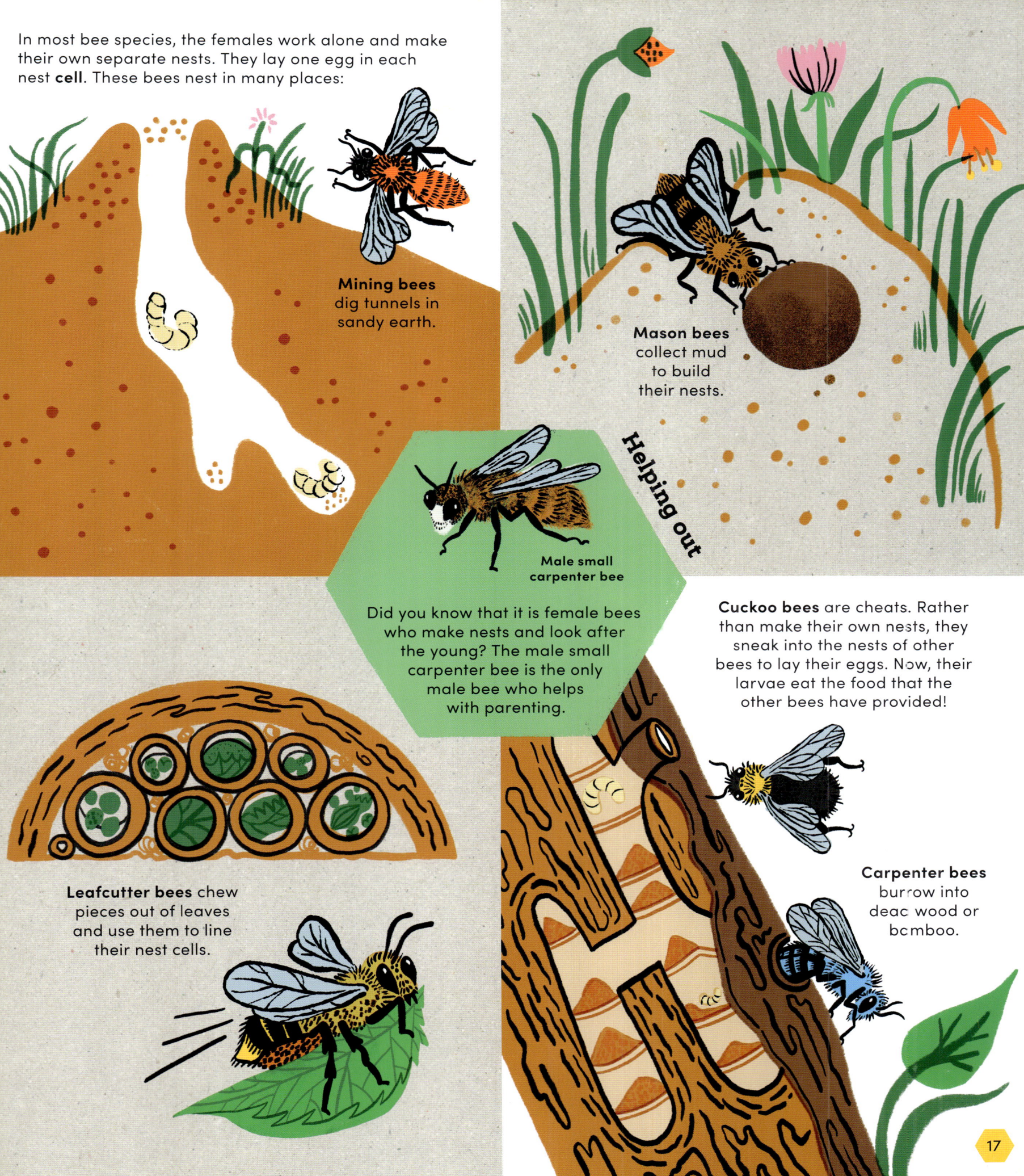

In most bee species, the females work alone and make their own separate nests. They lay one egg in each nest **cell**. These bees nest in many places:

Mining bees dig tunnels in sandy earth.

Mason bees collect mud to build their nests.

Helping out

Male small carpenter bee

Did you know that it is female bees who make nests and look after the young? The male small carpenter bee is the only male bee who helps with parenting.

Cuckoo bees are cheats. Rather than make their own nests, they sneak into the nests of other bees to lay their eggs. Now, their larvae eat the food that the other bees have provided!

Leafcutter bees chew pieces out of leaves and use them to line their nest cells.

Carpenter bees burrow into dead wood or bamboo.

17

What happens inside a hive?

Honeybees live in massive groups called colonies. All of the honeybees in a colony work together as a team.

Of course, every honeybee **colony** needs a home. Today, this is usually a wooden hive made by humans. The honeybees are free to come and go as they please, and then they zoom off to fields, gardens and other flowery places to find food.

The hive has three types of bee: worker, drone and queen.

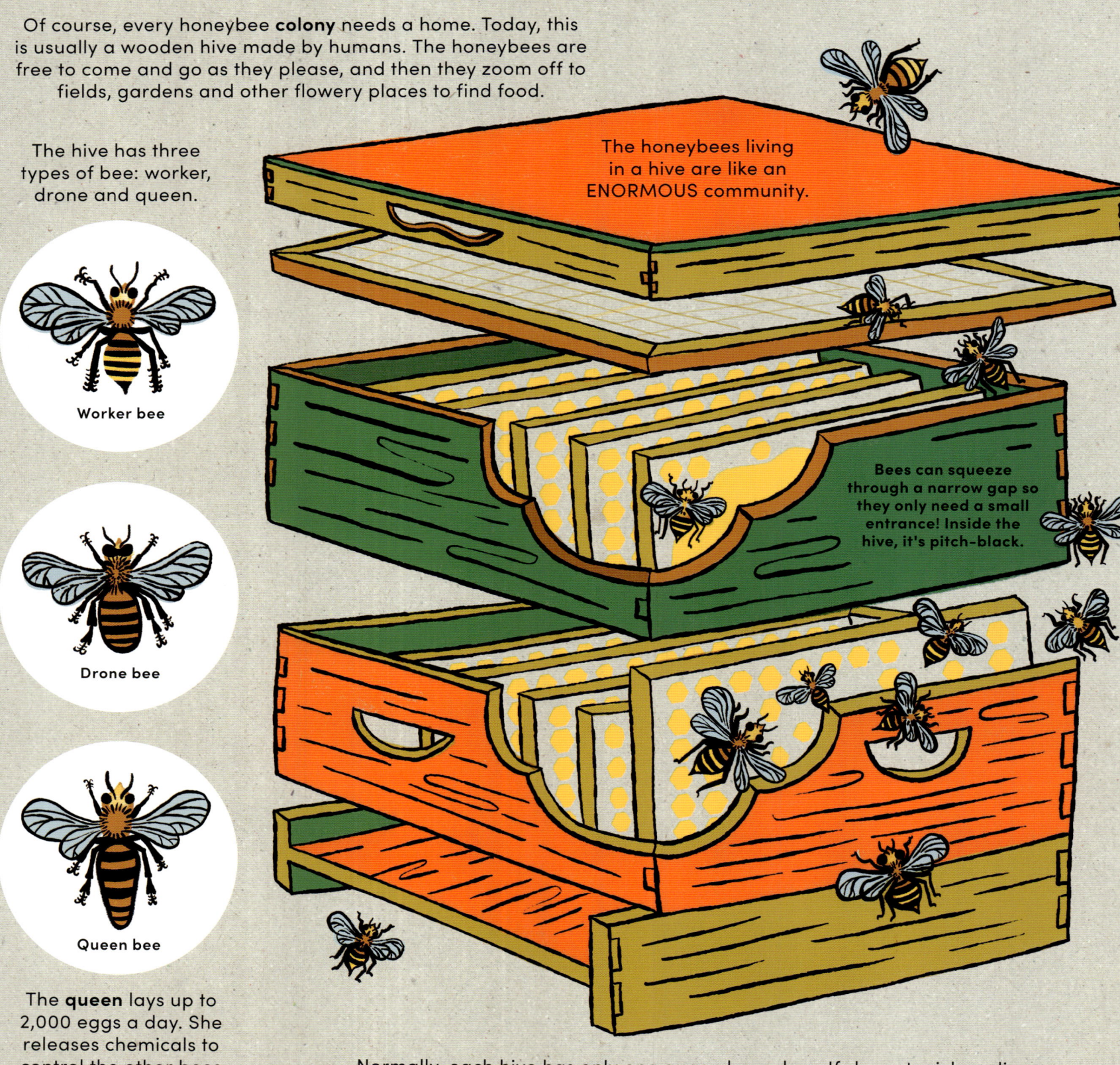

The honeybees living in a hive are like an ENORMOUS community.

Bees can squeeze through a narrow gap so they only need a small entrance! Inside the hive, it's pitch-black.

Worker bee

Drone bee

Queen bee

The **queen** lays up to 2,000 eggs a day. She releases chemicals to control the other bees in the **colony**. She lives for up to four years.

Normally, each hive has only one queen honeybee. If she gets sick or dies, the worker honeybees know what to do. They feed a special food called **royal jelly** to several of the hive's young bees. This turns them into new queens, one of which now takes over the hive. The other queens are killed or they fly off to start colonies of their own somewhere else.

Workers are all female, but unlike the queen, they don't lay eggs. There may be 50,000 workers, sometimes even more, who share many different jobs. They only live four to six weeks, in the busy summer months.

Worker honeybees are *always* busy! Between them, they do these jobs:

Clean the nest

Make honey

Defend the nest

Build and repair the nest

Search for food

Care for the eggs, young and queen

In the wild, honeybees nest in hollow trees.

Drones are the male bees. They have one task – leave the hive to find a queen and mate with her. They die soon afterwards.

Global bees

There are around 100 million hives around the world! They are home to 2 trillion honeybees – that's 2,000,000,000,000 buzzy bees!

19

How do bees make honey?

Honey is a golden, sugary liquid made by bees that live in colonies. They give it to the young bees and store it to eat at times of the year when there aren't many flowers to feed from.

Humans find honey delicious, too! Honeybees store so much honey in their hives that we can take some for ourselves, as long as we leave plenty for them to use.

But how do honeybees actually *make* their honey?

Worker honeybees also produce **beeswax**. They use this wonderful stuff to build the thousands of cells in their nest. The cells have six sides and fit together in a grid, which we call **honeycomb**. Some cells are used as honey factories. Some are for storing honey and the rest are nurseries, with one young bee in each cell.

1 Worker bees return to the nest with a stomach full of nectar.

2 They bring the nectar into their mouth and pass it to other workers.

3 These workers pack the nectar into tiny cells.

In Australia, people collect honey from wild **sugarbag bees**.

Bumblebees make small amounts of a sticky liquid a bit like honey. This 'sort-of honey' tastes nice and sweet, but it's impossible for humans to collect in the same way as honey.

4

The nectar loses most of its water and turns into honey.

Ancient bees

Did you know that the ancient Egyptians kept hives of honeybees? They believed that the bees were created from the tears of their Sun god, Ra.

Chatty bees

To make honey and do their other jobs, honeybees must work well as a team. So they 'talk' to each other all the time – but not with words! Instead, they send updates with chemicals and by shaking their body. They also do the **waggle dance**. These dance moves are a secret code that tell the other worker bees where flowers are.

Where do the other bees live?

Honeybees are not the only bees that live in large groups, or colonies. Some other bees form colonies too. Each colony is made up of a queen, female workers and male drones. It's an extraordinary way of life!

A **bumblebee** colony can have several hundred workers living in it. The queen bumblebee chooses where to build the nest, often among grass, under a rock or in an old mousehole.

When worker bumblebees visit flowers to gather pollen, they pack it into hairy baskets on their back legs. This allows the bees to carry heavy loads of pollen back to the nest, like someone carrying bags of shopping.

Wax pots for storing 'sort-of honey'

Some bumblebees take over nest boxes put up for birds. There are around 250 kinds of bumblebee, mainly found in cooler parts of the world.

In tropical areas, you will find colonies of **stingless bees**. These bees actually do have stingers, but they can't sting you. There are over 500 kinds of stingless bees, which nest in many different places:

Spiny-legged stingless bees are found in forests in South America. Their nests hang from branches high up in the trees and look like giant lumps of dry mud. A single nest may be home to more than 100,000 worker bees, meaning these are the biggest bee colonies on the planet!

Mopane bees are found in grasslands in Africa. The bees are tiny and dig their nests underground. They also nest inside **termite mounds**. Sometimes, people keep the bees in hives.

Mayan bees are found in forests in Central America. Usually, they nest in hollow trees or logs. The bees make tasty honey. Long ago, the Mayan people used to collect this honey, and it is still harvested today.

Why do bees have stings?

Ouch! If a bee stings you, it *really* hurts. Bees have many enemies that would love to eat them or the young in their nest, or steal their honey. So, bees have a painful sting to defend themselves and guard their colonies.

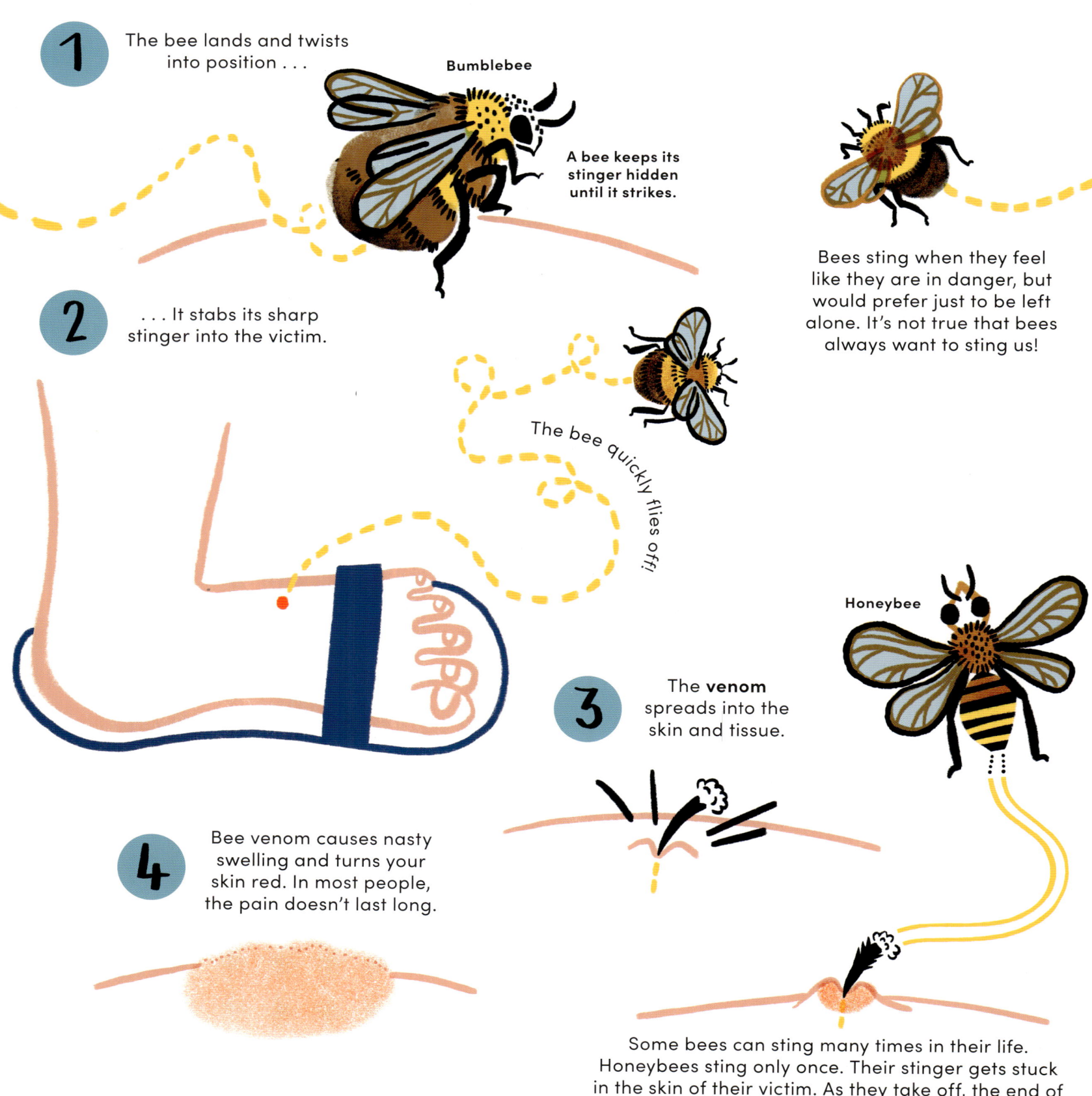

1 The bee lands and twists into position . . .

Bumblebee

A bee keeps its stinger hidden until it strikes.

Bees sting when they feel like they are in danger, but would prefer just to be left alone. It's not true that bees always want to sting us!

2 . . . It stabs its sharp stinger into the victim.

The bee quickly flies off!

3 The **venom** spreads into the skin and tissue.

Honeybee

4 Bee venom causes nasty swelling and turns your skin red. In most people, the pain doesn't last long.

Some bees can sting many times in their life. Honeybees sting only once. Their stinger gets stuck in the skin of their victim. As they take off, the end of their body is left behind, and they die.

Bee or wasp?

Bees and wasps are similar. But look closer… wasps often have smooth bodies.
Bees are much hairier so pollen sticks to their body.

Warning colours

Have you ever wondered why bees have stripes and bold colours? It's often a warning to other animals. Their colours send a message: "Don't touch me! I am armed and you'll regret it!"

Yellowjacket wasp

Honeybee

In Japan, honeybees have another secret weapon. Their worst enemy is the Asian hornet, a kind of wasp, and if it attacks, they swarm around it.

Buzz
Buzz
Buzz
Buzz
Buzz

Buzzing their wings to create heat, they burn the hornet to death.

Why do we need bees?

Thanks to bees, our beautiful green planet is full of flowers. Many flowering plants depend on bees to pollinate them. In turn, these plants provide food and homes for countless other animals. Bees are an essential part of the natural world.

Bees help us to grow much of the food we eat. They pollinate around two thirds of our crops, including lots of our favourite fruits, nuts and vegetables. They also pollinate plants that give us herbs, spices, medicines and the vegetable oils we use in cooking.

Honeybees pollinate more than 130 different crops. But we are helped by many other bees as well:

Orchard mason bees pollinate fruit trees.

Small carpenter bees pollinate avocados.

Alfalfa leafcutter bees pollinate carrots and some other fruits and vegetables.

Bumblebees pollinate crops such as tomatoes, cucumbers, blueberries and kiwi fruit.

Bees on the move

Every spring in California, USA, fleets of trucks take hives of honeybees to almond farms. When the bees have pollinated all of the almond trees in an area, their hives are packed up and they are trucked to the next farm.

Melipona bees pollinate vanilla flowers.

Without bees, Earth would be a very different place – and much less colourful.

Bees themselves are also on the menu!

Many predators rely on them for food.

The **European bee-eater** is a superb flyer. This colourful bird chases bees and catches them in mid-air.

Using its powerful claws, the **honey badger** smashes bee nests apart to eat the young bees and honey.

The **beewolf** is a large wasp that hunts bees, stings them to stop them moving, then feeds them to its young.

How can we help bees?

All of us can play our part to help bees.

Honeybees are not in trouble, because **beekeepers** look after them. But wild bees are losing their habitats as we cut down forests and use land for farming, roads and houses. The chemicals we spray on fields and gardens kill them, too. Climate change can also be dangerous for bees. It changes when and where plants flower, which leaves them without food when they need it.

Do **Provide nest sites**

Bees need somewhere to nest. You could leave a patch of bare soil for digger and mining bees to use. Or you could put up a 'bee hotel', which is the bee version of a nest box for birds. Mason and leafcutter bees love bee hotels!

Do **Plant more flowers**

It's best to plant a variety of flowers that different bees will feed from. Even a single flowerpot or a planter on a windowsill can attract bees.

Do **Rescue a bee**

If you see a bee moving slowly on the ground, it might be hungry. Put a spoon or capful of sugary water beside the bee. With luck, it will sip some and soon recover.

Do Bee an expert

One way to help bees is by learning more about them – and you have made a great start by reading this book! There are many mysteries about bees that are still waiting for an answer. Take sleep, for example. We know that bees go to sleep, but we don't yet know if they dream. One day, a bee expert of the future may find out . . .

Don't Use pesticides

Pesticides are chemicals that kill insect 'pests'. The problem is, they kill bees as well.

World Bee Day

World Bee Day is held every year on 20th May. There are events around the world to celebrate bees and how brilliant they are.

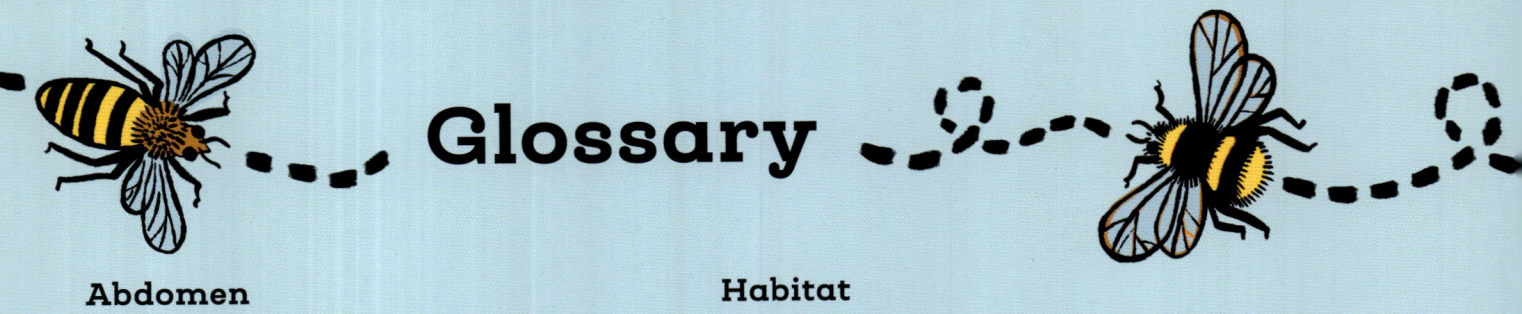

Glossary

Abdomen

One of the three main sections in the body of an insect. It's the last section, after the thorax.

Antennae

Sensitive feelers on an animal's head that detect touch and smell.

Beekeeper

A person who looks after a hive of honeybees and collects some of their honey.

Colony

A group of the same species of animal living together. Insects that live in colonies often share a nest.

Continent

A huge area of land. Earth has seven continents, which are separated by oceans, rivers or mountains.

Crops

Plants we grow for food or as a source of other useful products.

Electro sense

The ability to detect electric fields. Animals that have this sense often use it to find food.

Exoskeleton

A hard outer skeleton that supports an animal's body and protects it. Insects have an exoskeleton.

Habitat

A particular type of place where living things are found, such as a forest, garden or pond.

Honeycomb

A piece of beeswax produced by honeybees. It's made of cells, which have six sides and are arranged in a grid, like tiles on a floor.

Invertebrate

An animal with no backbone. Insects are invertebrates.

Larva

An early growth stage in the life of some animals, such as insects.

Mineral

A type of nutrient that a living thing needs to grow and stay healthy.

Nectar

A sugary liquid produced by flowers. Bees collect nectar to make honey.

Nerves

Bundles of cells that act like cables to carry messages around the body of an animal.

Pesticides

Chemicals used to kill insects or plants that people view as pests.

Pigment

A substance that gives colour to other things.

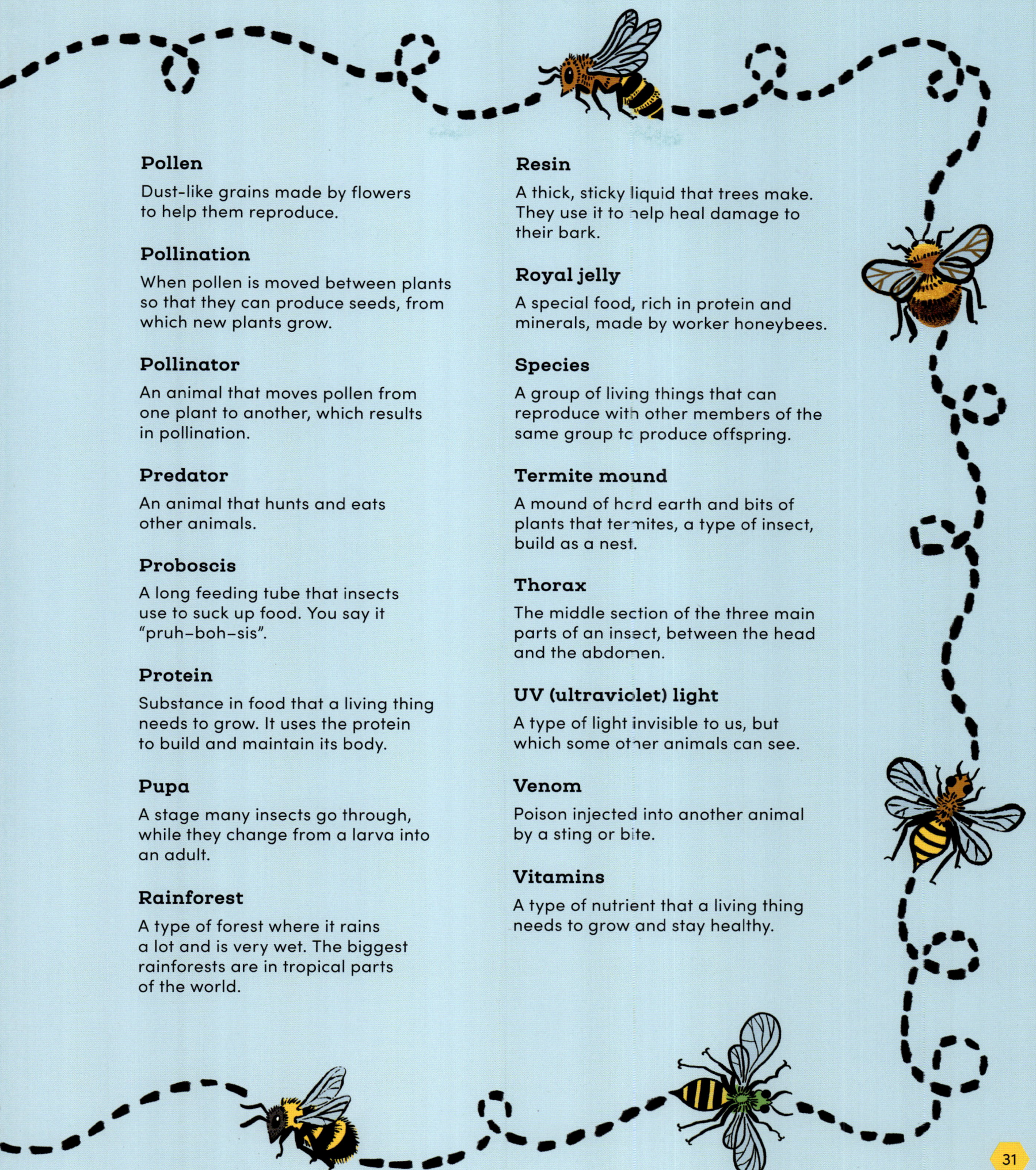

Pollen

Dust-like grains made by flowers to help them reproduce.

Pollination

When pollen is moved between plants so that they can produce seeds, from which new plants grow.

Pollinator

An animal that moves pollen from one plant to another, which results in pollination.

Predator

An animal that hunts and eats other animals.

Proboscis

A long feeding tube that insects use to suck up food. You say it "pruh–boh–sis".

Protein

Substance in food that a living thing needs to grow. It uses the protein to build and maintain its body.

Pupa

A stage many insects go through, while they change from a larva into an adult.

Rainforest

A type of forest where it rains a lot and is very wet. The biggest rainforests are in tropical parts of the world.

Resin

A thick, sticky liquid that trees make. They use it to help heal damage to their bark.

Royal jelly

A special food, rich in protein and minerals, made by worker honeybees.

Species

A group of living things that can reproduce with other members of the same group to produce offspring.

Termite mound

A mound of hard earth and bits of plants that termites, a type of insect, build as a nest.

Thorax

The middle section of the three main parts of an insect, between the head and the abdomen.

UV (ultraviolet) light

A type of light invisible to us, but which some other animals can see.

Venom

Poison injected into another animal by a sting or bite.

Vitamins

A type of nutrient that a living thing needs to grow and stay healthy.

Index

A
Antennae 7, 14–15, 30

B
Bees

    Bumble 9, 13, 15, 21–22, 24, 26
    Cactus 9
    Carpenter 9, 11, 17, 26
    Honey 8, 15, 18–22, 24–28
    Leafcutter 17, 26, 28
    Long-legged oil 8
    Mason 17, 26, 28
    Mayan 23
    Melipona 27
    Mining 6, 17, 28
    Mini-fairy 8
    Mopane 23
    Orchid 8–10
    Stingless 23
    Sugarbag 21
    Sweat 7, 11–12
    Vulture 11
    Wallace's giant 8
Beekeeper 28, 30
Beeswax 20
Birds 13, 22, 27

C
Climate change 28
Colony 18, 22, 30

D
Drones 18–19, 22

E
Earth 8, 27
Eggs 16–19

F
Farming 26–28
Flowers 10–15, 18, 20–22, 26–28
Fruit 26

H
Hive 18–21, 23, 27
Honey 19–24, 27
Honeycomb 20, 30

L
Larva 16–17, 30
Leaves 17

M
Mud 17, 23

N
Nectar 10–12, 14–16, 20–21, 30
Nest 15, 17, 19, 20, 22–24, 27, 28

P
Pesticides 29–30
Plants 12–13, 15, 26, 28
Pollen 10, 12–16, 22, 25, 31

Q
Queen 18–19, 22

R
Royal jelly 18, 31

S
Sting 6, 23–24, 27

T
Trees 19, 23, 26–27

V
Vegetables 26

W
Waggle dance 21
Wasps 13, 25, 27
Wings 6, 13, 16, 25
Workers 18–23